MW00896164

GREAT BUSINESS STORIES

HENRY FORD
AND
FORD

MICHAEL POLLARD

OTHER TITLES IN THE SERIES
Anita Roddick and The Body Shop by Paul Brown
Akio Morita and Sony by David Marshall
Bill Gates and Microsoft by David Marshall
Coco Chanel and Chanel by David Bond
George Eastman and Kodak by Peter Brooke-Ball

Picture Credits
AKG London: 18/19, 44-45, 54; **Allsport:** 18-19/Pascal Rondeau; **Ann Ronan/Image Select:** 6;
Ford UK: Cover, 16, 20, 27 (below), 28 (both), 37 (below), 56 (right), 57 (both); **Ford USA:** 21,
25, 30 (both), 32, 34-35 (all), 37 (above), 38, 41, 43, 48, 50 (both), 55, 59, 60 (above); **Images:** 4-
5, 39 (both), 48-49, 52-53, 53 (left), 58; **National Motor Museum:** 29, 31, 56 (centre), 60
(below); **Popperfoto:** 7 (above), 15, 24, 36, 40, 46, 51; **Quadrant:** 42; **Range/Bettmann:** 7
(below), 8, 9, 10, 13, 14, 22-23 (all), 26, 27 (above), 47, 56 (left); **Spectrum:** 11, 17, 53 (right).

The Publishers have been unable to contact the copyright holder of *My Life and Work* by Henry
Ford for the extracts used in this book, and would be grateful for any information.

Published in Great Britain in 1995
by Exley Publications Ltd,
16 Chalk Hill, Watford,
Herts WD1 4BN, United Kingdom.

**A copy of the CIP data is available from the
British Library on request.**

ISBN 1-85015-493-7

Editor: Helen Lanz
Editorial assistant: Alison MacTier
Picture editors: Alex Goldberg and James Clift of
Image Select
Typeset by Delta Print, Watford, Herts, U.K.
Printed at Oriental Press, – UAE.

HENRY FORD
AND
FORD

MICHAEL POLLARD

In September 1908, an advertisement in American newspapers and magazines announced the forthcoming arrival on the market of a new car.

The newcomer, the advertisement said, was "powerful, speedy and enduring – a car that looks good and is as good as it looks. Better features or as high-grade materials cannot be found in any other car at any price. A better car is not and cannot be made."

The new model, the advertisement went on, was to be sold at $850. This was "several hundred dollars less than the lowest of the rest."

No doubt many readers glanced at the advertisement, smiled at its extravagant claims, and turned the page. How could a manufacturer sell a car several hundred dollars cheaper than anyone else and at the same time claim that it was the best on the

Previous page: Henry Ford would have appreciated the modern car production line with its robotic tools and computer-controlled operations. He believed that speed and efficiency of production were the key to success in industry – and he was proved right.

Below: Although only two years old, the Model T of 1910 was already a runaway winner. At one stage, Henry Ford had to ask dealers not to take any more orders because the factory was working as hard as it could. Consequently he was already thinking of ways to increase production.

market? It didn't make sense. In any case, most newspaper and magazine readers had never even thought of the possibility of owning a car. They still regarded cars as toys, not to be taken seriously.

They didn't know that the advertisement heralded at least two revolutions – a revolution in the American, and ultimately the world's, way of life, and a revolution in the manufacturing industry. For the car being advertised – the "Ford Four Cylinder, Twenty Horse Power, Five Passenger Touring Car" – was the Model T. It was a car that would change the world, and it was the brainchild of Henry Ford.

A car for the multitude

The Model T was different from any other car that had been made before. It not only looked different from other cars – it was made with a new kind of customer in mind. From the start, it had been designed as a practical and reliable means of travel for ordinary people – the people that Henry Ford called "the great multitude."

Despite what the advertisement said, the Model T was not a handsome-looking car. Ford's design made no concessions to style. Nor was it powerful. It was a no-frills mechanical workhorse for everyday use – a "universal car." This, Ford believed, was what people were waiting for. And within a short space of time he was proved right.

The Model T went on sale on October 1, 1908. That day saw the achievement of a ten-year-old dream for Henry Ford. Over the next nineteen years, until the Model T finally ceased production, it was to meet the dreams, too, of millions of farmers and small-town families across the United States – and thousands in Europe – who wanted a cheap, reliable, all-purpose means of travel. Commercially, the Model T was the most successful single car ever made, and over fifteen million were sold worldwide. This was almost as many as were sold during the same period by all other car manufacturers together.

Above: Even as a young boy Henry Ford had begun to show an interest in mechanics.
Below: The decisive Battle of Gettysburg of the American Civil War began on July 1, 1863, and lasted for two days.

Two dates in July

Henry Ford was born on July 30, 1863, on a farm at Greenfield, near Dearborn in Michigan, about nine miles (14.5km) from Detroit. He was the eldest of six children in a family of four boys and two girls. His parents had emigrated to the United States from Ireland almost twenty years before.

For all such families, life was a struggle. Henry's father, William Ford, was more successful than many Michigan farmers, but he had earned his success with endless hard work. He owned some primitive horse-drawn machinery, but much of farming was still a matter of hard physical work.

The year and even the month of Henry Ford's birth was a significant one in American history. For two years, the United States had been torn apart by the American Civil War. In the struggle between the Northern and Southern states, over half a million men were to die before it was over. Although the Civil War dragged on until 1865, July 1863 saw one of its fiercest battles, at Gettysburg. Over six thousand men died there, but it proved to be a turning point. The Southern army, commanded by

In the 1860s, the transcontinental railway line between eastern and western states was built by hundreds of construction crews. Trestle bridges, built from timber felled on the spot, carried the track across rivers and gullies. Its construction speeded up the development of the mid western United States by pioneer farming families.

General Robert E. Lee, was forced to retreat, and from then on there was no doubt that the North would eventually win the war. The United States, instead of being two groups of warring states, would become united again.

It was the changes that came with the unification of the United States that indirectly contributed to Henry Ford's later success.

America grows

The Civil War created a huge demand for uniforms, firearms, and munitions, resulting in faster and more efficient production. After the war, the manufacturing skills developed to cope with this demand were turned to peaceful purposes. At the same time, railways were opening up the undeveloped states of America's Midwest. In 1865 work began on linking the East Coast states by rail with the West Coast. The line was completed four years later. Two other significant industrial developments took place around the same time. The open-hearth process for producing steel was developed, making the production of high-grade steel easier and cheaper. And in 1865, the world's first oil

pipeline was laid in the Allegheny River valley in Pennsylvania in order to carry the product of the new oil industry.

Alongside these industrial developments there was a huge growth in farming. The great corn and cattle lands of the West were opened up by the railway, and over the next fifty years hundreds of thousands of settler families – many of them immigrants from Europe – moved westward to set up their homesteads. These families and their children were to form an important market for the products of American industry – including Henry Ford's cars. The foundations of the United States' future were laid.

Harvesting by mechanical reaper was invented in 1840 but only the most prosperous farmers could afford to invest in it. During Ford's lifetime the whole process of farm work would be revolutionized by the increasing use of machines.

Machine mad

Growing up on a remote Michigan farm, Henry Ford knew little of all this – but he soon showed signs that he belonged to a new generation of Americans interested more in the industrial future than in the agricultural past. Like most pioneer farmers, his father, William, hoped that his eldest son would join him on the farm, enable it to expand, and eventually take it over. But Henry proved a disappointment. He hated farm work and did everything he could to

"Even when I was very young I suspected that much might somehow be done in a better way. That is what took me into mechanics – although my mother always said that I was a born mechanic."

Henry Ford, *from* My Life and Work.

avoid it. It was not that he was lazy. Far from it. Give him a mechanical job to do, from mending the hinges of a gate to sharpening tools, and he would set to work eagerly. It was the daily life of the farm, with its repetitive tasks, that frustrated him. "What a waste it is," he was to write years later, remembering his work in the fields, "for a human being to spend hours and days behind a slowly moving team of horses."

Henry was excited by the possibilities for the future that were being opened up by developments in technology that could free farmers like his father from wasteful and boring toil. But these developments, in Henry's boyhood, had touched farming hardly at all and farmers went on doing things in the way they had always done. Low profits, the uncertainties of the weather, and farmers' instinctive resistance to change prevented all but the richest and most far-sighted farmers from taking advantage of the new age of machines.

So Henry turned his attention elsewhere. When he was twelve he became almost obsessively interested in clocks and watches. Like most children before and since, he became fascinated by peering into the workings of a timepiece and watching the movement of ratchets and wheels, springs and pendulums. Soon he was repairing clocks and watches for friends, working at a bench he built in his bedroom.

Breaking away

Henry had never got on well with his father. Not one to show his feelings, William Ford seemed interested in his son only as a helper on the farm. In Henry's eyes, his father had wasted his life in remorseless hard work for little reward, and Henry had no intention of repeating the pattern. Henry's mother, Mary Ford, was a more loving influence.

From his parents, Henry learned to love the countryside and understand it through careful observation. Mary also taught him, by example, the virtue of thrift, a lesson that was to stay with him all his life. For farming families like the Fords, thrift was often the key to survival. Henry was brought up

As the mother of six and a farmer's wife, Henry Ford's mother would have had to work very hard to look after her family and carry out all her domestic duties. She had a great influence on Henry, and her premature death cast a shadow over his childhood.

to hate waste, dislike any kind of luxury, and regard hard work – provided it produced results – as life's main purpose.

In 1876, Henry suffered a grievous blow. Mary died in childbirth. There was now no reason for him to stay on the farm, and he resolved to get away as soon as he could. Three years later, he took a job as a mechanic in Detroit. By this time steam engines had joined clocks and watches as objects of Henry's fascination.

According to an account given by Henry himself, he first saw a steam-driven road locomotive one day in 1877 when he and his father, in their horse-drawn farm wagon, met one on the road. The locomotive driver stopped to let the wagon pass, and Henry jumped down and went to him with a barrage of technical questions about the engine's performance. From then on, for a while, Henry became infatuated with steam engines. Making and installing them was the business of the Detroit workshop that he joined at the age of sixteen.

Moonlighting

Henry stayed with an aunt during this time and worked at the steam engine workshop during the day. In the evenings he moonlighted as a watch repairer –

"He had, from childhood, an impelling urge to make things; to take materials and turn them into something that moved, or into tools that helped to make other things. That urge guided his whole life, and is probably ninety per cent of the secret of Henry Ford's success."

C. L. Caldwell,
from Henry Ford.

11

more out of interest and to fill his time than because he needed the money.

Over the next three years, he toyed with the idea of setting up his own business as a watchmaker, but when he had worked out the costs and the likely market he rejected it. He decided that he would need to make huge numbers of watches to keep the price down – but "watches were not universal necessities, and therefore people generally would not buy them." In those days, people did not need to wear watches. Clocks were displayed on public buildings such as town halls and churches, factories, and, in farming districts, the sun provided all the timekeeping they needed. But Henry's comment shows that already he had in his mind the idea that was to make his fortune – if you can find a way of making something that everyone wants cheaply enough, you have the beginnings of a thriving business. To this, he would later add a refinement – people do not always know what they want until you tell them.

On the back burner

For the time being, however, Henry's ambitions had to be put on the back burner. In 1884, when Henry was twenty-one, his father gave him forty acres (sixteen hectares) of timbered land to tempt him back to rural life. Henry accepted the offer and for the next few years threw himself into managing his timber, running a sawmill, and building a house.

During this time Henry met a local girl, Clara Bryant. Henry was not like any of the other young men with whom Clara associated. He was rather serious and intense. He didn't approve of drinking or smoking. It is said he only learned to dance in order to be able to meet Clara – such a pastime had not interested him before. But Clara found that she was attracted to Henry's intensity and enjoyed being involved in discussing his business ideas and dreams. Romance blossomed, and on April 11, 1888, the couple were married.

Once they had settled, however, farm life began to bore Henry again. He had found a new technical interest. In 1879, an American lawyer, George

"There is an immense amount to be learned simply by tinkering with things. It is not possible to learn from books how nearly everything is made – and a real mechanic ought to know how nearly everything is made. Machines are to a mechanic what books are to a writer. He gets ideas from them, and if he has any brains he will apply those ideas."

Henry Ford,
from My Life and Work.

Baldwin Selden, had designed a motor car using a type of fuel engine invented eighteen years earlier by the German Nikolaus Otto. Selden was not an engineer and did not actually build his car, but he filed a patent that would prevent anyone else from copying his ideas without paying him a fee. This, however, did not stop others, both amateur and professional engineers, from experimenting with fuel-driven cars. News of their efforts was carried in the technical magazines that Henry Ford read avidly. Henry felt desperately frustrated and trapped on the farm, away from the city and the new developments taking place. At last, in 1891, he had had enough. In the late summer of that year, he and Clara loaded their furniture onto a wagon and left for Detroit.

The American lawyer George Baldwin Selden, pictured below with his son, Henry, made his money by granting licences to his manufacturers in return for a fee. Henry Ford and other car makers challenged Selden's exclusive right to grant licences in a long, hard-fought court case. Eventually Selden lost, and his name was virtually "written out" of the history of the car industry.

Responsibilities

A chance meeting with an old co-worker led to a job for Henry as an engineer at the Edison Detroit Electricity Company, the leading force in another new industry. Power stations were being built and cables being laid in all of the United States' major cities; the age of electricity had dawned. But although Henry

Henry Ford began to build his first car, the Quadricycle in a workshop such as this. The photograph was taken from the viewpoint of the wall which Ford had to demolish in order to take his new invention on its maiden trip.

quickly learned the ropes of his new job – so quickly that within four years he was chief engineer at the Detroit power plant – his interest in fuel engines had come to dominate his life. At first in the kitchen of his and Clara's home, and later in a shed at the back of their house, he spent his spare time in the evenings trying to build an engine to his own design.

Meanwhile, Henry's domestic responsibilities had increased. In November 1893, Clara gave birth to their first and only child, Edsel.

Learning the hard way

Henry learned the hard way what a slow, painstaking business it was to build an engine by hand from scratch. Every piece of every component had to be fashioned individually, checked and rechecked, and tested. Every problem had to be worried over and solved by the builder. To ease the burden, Henry joined forces with another mechanic, Jim Bishop. Even so, it was two years before they had succeeded in building a working car. It was an ungainly-looking vehicle, mounted on bicycle wheels and driven by a rubber belt that connected the engine to the rear wheels. Henry called it the "Quadricycle."

The first Ford on the road

The first trial of Henry's car, in June 1896, began with an anticlimax. He and Jim Bishop had worked through the night to get it ready for the road, and it was almost dawn before they finished. It was pouring with rain. Should they put off the trial until daylight and fine weather? No. They couldn't wait. They pushed the car up to the shed door … only to find that it was too big to go through. Howling with impatience and frustration, Henry picked up an axe and began to demolish the front wall of the shed. And so it was, at about four in the morning, that Ford's first car made its maiden trip through the wet streets of Detroit.

The sight of "Crazy Ford," as he was known, driving about in his weird-looking vehicle, sometimes with Clara and Edsel, now three years old, became a familiar one in Detroit. Already, Henry was thinking of improvements. To finance them, he sold his first car for $200 and started to build a second.

A fateful choice

Henry Ford was soon faced with a difficult decision. While he was quietly building his car in the shed behind his home, the Edison company had taken no interest in his after-work activities. What employees did in their spare time was their own affair. But once Henry started driving his car around, and once it was known that he had sold one car and proposed to build another, his employers began to wonder if he was giving enough attention to his day job. They put him to the test by offering him a promotion to general manager of the Detroit plant – provided he gave up tinkering with cars.

The promotion would mean a big increase in his salary – enough to enable him to buy new tools and materials, rent a larger workshop, build an improved version of his car, to say nothing of providing a better home for Clara and Edsel. But building another car was of course the one thing that he would be prevented from doing. The young Ford family had to live, but no one working on his own could hope to make a living building cars. If he was to become a car-maker, Ford would need partners, money with which to establish the business and buy tools and materials, and a regular income.

Ford drove his Quadricycle, shown here on one of its first trips in 1896, as often as possible to attract publicity. His achievement did not meet with everyone's approval, however. To many, it seemed crazy for a skilled engineer to devote so much time to a machine that would never "catch on."

A decision is made

After ten sleepless nights spent worrying over this problem, Ford found backers and made his decision. With investment from a handful of local businessmen, led by a Detroit timber merchant, William Murphy, the Detroit Automobile Company was formed in 1899. Ford, now thirty-six, resigned from the electricity company and became the new company's chief engineer. But there was a price to pay. He took a cut in salary.

Storms over Detroit

Although Ford was by now adept at car engineering, he had little first-hand experience of the business world. Building cars in the evenings as a hobby took no real account of the costs of either materials or manual work. Ford had been glad to get $200 for his first effort – but that was nowhere near its real value in terms of his time and skill. The complex process of costing a manufactured product, taking into account materials, hours of work, overheads such as rent and power, and above all a profit margin from which the investors in the company could be paid a dividend and which could also be used to develop the company's business, was all new to him. This was one reason why business life came as a great shock to him.

Henry Ford had to struggle to establish mass-market car production in his day. Today, however, car making is a major worldwide industry involving international cooperation in design, engineering, manufacture, and marketing. The number of cars waiting to be loaded for export from the docks in Osaka, Japan, illustrates just how successful mass-market car production is today.

Another was the emergence of a side of Ford's nature that he was to demonstrate many times in his life. He was an individualist who found it difficult to work with other people. Unless his business partners or employees agreed with him 100%, he believed they were against him. Just such a combination of characteristics as Henry Ford had – genius in one particular aspect, together with an arrogant self-confidence – has ruined many a promising enterprise. Business decisions are often a matter of compromise, of weighing up different options and choosing one of them. Successful businesses can often stem from the foresight, talent, and determination of a single character, but their survival can also depend on a combination of talents of a number of people working together with a common sense of purpose. Ford believed that he was always

"Every generation has its own problems; it ought to find out its own solutions. There is no use in our living if we can't do things better than our fathers did."
Henry Ford, 1925.

Motor racing was an early interest of Henry Ford's. Although cars built for racing were never suitable for everyday use, he recognized the publicity to be gained by racing wins. The competitive nature of motor sport also makes it an ideal arena for engineering development. The car industry has continued to spend heavily on racing and rallying, the equivalent sport using production models.

right. If pushed, he would simply ignore evidence that conflicted with his own ideas.

For their part, his backers were impatient. Fifteen months went by. Only a handful of cars had been produced, and the company was heavily in debt. At last, the other directors' nerve broke. In November 1900 they wound up the company, sold its materials, parts, and equipment for scrap, and sacked Henry Ford. He did not attend the board meeting to hear the sentence. "If they ask for me," he told a colleague, "tell them I had to go out of town." If there was one thing that Henry Ford could not bear to hear, it was the suggestion that he had been a failure.

It was the lowest point yet in Ford's life. He had no job. He had, though he may not have admitted it even to himself, failed the Detroit Automobile Company. He could not afford to keep a home for his

wife and son and they went to live with his father, now retired from the farm and living in Detroit. Clara began to worry about her husband's health and the family's future.

A new venture

But Ford bounced back. Within a few months he had persuaded five of the investors in the failed Detroit Automobile Company to back him in business again, as the Henry Ford Company – designing and building a racing car.

There is a mystery about this phase of Henry's life. His story, years later, was that he was really only interested in producing a low-priced car for the "great multitude," but built racing cars instead because that was what the other directors wanted.

A rare early picture of Ford preparing for a motor race. His engineering knowledge of racing cars was used to improve the designs of his family cars – for example, in his introduction of disc brakes to all British-built family cars after 1960.

Their story was the exact opposite. Whatever the truth, the racing cars that Henry built were certainly successful. Driving one of them, he became the American motor racing champion in 1901. Three years later, another Ford racer broke the world record for the mile in 39.4 seconds, a then-incredible speed of 91.4 miles (147km) per hour. But racing cars were not what Ford was to become famous for.

The Henry Ford Company lasted for sixteen months until, once again, Ford fell out with his partners. They continued with the company, choosing a new name which was to become famous at the luxury end of the motor industry – Cadillac. Meanwhile, Ford continued to build racing cars in partnership with a young racing cyclist, Tom Cooper, who had made a fortune in prize money. This alliance, too, ended quickly. Henry Ford was beginning to look like bad news. He may be a brilliant mechanic, it was said, but his trouble was that he just couldn't get along with people.

Ready-to-buy

While he was working on his racing cars, Ford, now approaching forty, had also been thinking. By the early 1900s, there were plenty of engineers capable of producing some kind of working car to order. What if, instead of waiting for some rich customer to place an order for a car, a manufacturer were to produce cars that could be bought "off the shelf" in the same way as people bought other things? While he struggled to master the mechanics of car-making, Henry Ford began to shape his vision of the car industry of the future, and by 1903 his ideas were more clearly formed. This industry would lure customers into showrooms instead of waiting for them to call. It would offer them cars they could drive away there and then. And it would make the ownership of a car so attractive, even essential, that every family would want one. By building cars in larger numbers, it would be possible to bring down the price to a generally affordable figure. Also, by producing in mass numbers, Ford's aim of buying "off the shelf" would be achievable.

These were revolutionary ideas in the motor industry of the time. Twenty years had gone by since two German engineers, Gottlieb Daimler and Karl Benz, had independently produced cars powered by a fuel-driven engine. Both had set up companies that were producing cars commercially and within a few years had granted licences to manufacturers in other countries. But the motor industry that had grown up produced cars for the rich. Each car was hand-built by highly-skilled craftsmen, in the same painstaking way as Henry Ford had built his first models. Ford's dream was to make every family a motoring family.

The rules of business

Experience had taught Henry Ford an important lesson. Building cars was one thing, selling them another. For most of the population, cars were for other people – fast cars for the young, stately cars for the rich. The trick was to make everyone realize that motoring could be for them too.

In other words, the idea of car ownership must be

Henry Ford recognized that a good relationship between dealer and customer was vital for future business. He aimed to hold on to his customers when they bought their next car, and to make owning a Ford a family habit. This policy is still reflected today in the company's high standard of customer care, frequent communication with existing and potential Ford motorists, and the aim of making visiting a Ford showroom, whether to buy a car or have it serviced, a pleasant and friendly experience.

The founding fathers of the Ford Motor Company, James Couzens (below) and Henry Ford (opposite).

marketed. A generation earlier, Isaac Merrit Singer had, by clever marketing, persuaded hundreds of thousands of American women that a sewing-machine was an essential piece of equipment for every home, and freed them from hours of concentrated toil with the needle. It was true that a motor car was a far more complex – and more expensive – product than a sewing-machine, but the same principles could be applied.

So hand in hand with Henry Ford's ideas for volume car production went his growing realization that the public must be tempted, even persuaded, into buying. As shown by the example of other products made by mass production, prices would be progressively lowered, thereby making the product accessible to even more customers.

However, another discovery Ford had made was that the financing of volume car production was more complex than he had anticipated. Almost all the costs are "up front" – in other words, they have to be paid before a single car is sold. A factory must be built or rented, money must be spent on design and testing, tools and equipment must be bought, materials must be obtained, workers must be paid. This was the problem that had put the Detroit Automobile Company so heavily in debt – large sums of money being spent, and only a handful of cars produced.

A new beginning

By 1903, Henry Ford had built up a reputation around Detroit but it was not a good one. He had fallen out with three sets of backers. He was obstinate and self-regarding. He walked away from trouble instead of staying on and seeing it through.

But there was one man in Detroit who had faith in Ford. He was the city's leading coal merchant, Alexander Malcolmson. He had been impressed with Ford's racing cars, and in 1903 he suggested that they should form a company, with a handful of Malcolmson's business associates, to produce a "commercial automobile." The new car would be designed for sale to the growing number of everyday motorists, rather than to racing enthusiasts. On 16 June that year the new company – the Ford Motor Company – was born, with Malcolmson as president and Henry Ford as vice-president. One of the smaller shareholders was Malcolmson's accountant, James Couzens, who joined the Ford company as its general manager and was to play a key role in its early history.

Left: Ford's initial investment in his motor company was to the share value of $25,500, as shown on the original share certificate.

Almost at once, a dispute broke out between Ford and his new backers. He wanted to produce the new car entirely "in house" to his own design, with the company making all the parts. In order to put a product on the market quickly, and so get some of their outlay back, the others wanted the car to be assembled from parts bought in from outside. Couzens could be just as obstinate as Ford, and the idea of using bought-in parts finally won.

Connections abroad

The first Ford cars were built from the chassis, the base frame, upwards by teams of two or three mechanics working on a group of four cars at a time. "Stock runners" brought parts from the warehouse as they were needed. For the skilled mechanics, there was a lot of stooping and stretching, which slowed

the work down, and a good deal of waiting around while one operation was finished before moving on to the next.

As he watched all this activity on the factory floor, Ford began to realize that there must be a more efficient way of building cars. Waiting time was wasted time for which the company was paying, an idea that offended the principles of thrift that Ford had learned all those years ago on the farm.

A later improvement on Ford factory production was to assemble the cars on stands or benches that could be moved along from one team of workers to the next. This had increased efficiency and productivity, but the cars were still largely hand-built. At that time there was no other way of organizing car assembly. There were no standardized parts, and so each car had to be built individually.

Despite these problems, in its first year the Ford Motor Company managed to build over six hundred of its Model A cars. Model A was followed by improved versions – B, C, F, K, N, R, and S – as Henry struggled for better performance and reliability. (The missing letters represent experimental models that never reached the production stage.)

Within months of the founding of the Ford Motor Company in the United States, the Model A attracted attention from abroad. Barely six months after the company was established, two Model A cars had found their way across the Atlantic to Britain, where a man named Percival Perry had acquired the right to sell Ford cars for the next five years. International demand grew for the company's products and by the following year, 1904, Ford's Model A had been exported to Canada and Australia. In the same year, Ford Motor Company itself established a base in Canada.

A dream of the future

As a self-taught engineer, Henry was unable to read an engineering drawing. He worked by instinct, and claimed to be able to tell whether a part was well designed by holding it in his hands. But this naturally held up progress and was a source of frustration to

his partners and colleagues. The individual-style production raised costs, so that as one Ford model succeeded the next, the price began to creep up to the luxury car level. Among luxury car makers there was fierce competition, and Ford had little to offer that other manufacturers could not do as well or even better. Indeed, compared with some of the splendid cars that were now being produced, Ford's looked dull and cumbersome.

Once the Ford Motor Company started to become established, Henry Ford returned to his dream of making a car for the "great multitude." His vision was of a plain, down-to-earth, no-nonsense vehicle that could cope with the rough, rutted roads of America's farming states and even bump over dug-up fields without trouble. With this in mind, it should have higher clearance from the ground than most cars of the time. It should be simple enough technically to be repaired and maintained by farm mechanics using everyday tools. It should be cheap, and it should last, as farmers expected their equipment to do. This idea was to turn into the Model T.

Without waiting to discuss the idea with Malcolmson or the other directors, Ford announced his plan in the spring of 1905 to the Detroit newspapers. He would, he said, build ten thousand cars to sell at $400 each. Not surprisingly, there was

Opposite: Despite his famous saying that "history is bunk," Ford valued the past. He restored the farm where he was born in Dearborn, Michigan, and built an old-world village around it. At the same time, he fixed his eyes on the future. As early as the 1920s, when commercial flying was in its infancy, the Dearborn site included an airport. Today, the world headquarters in Dearborn (above) is the main base for a global system of electronic communications.

Henry Ford, pictured at the wheel of a Model T outside the first Ford Motor Company showroom soon after the company was launched. He is credited with the decision that made driving on the right of the road almost universal. Before the car was developed, there was no "rule of the road." The car seen here has its wheel on the right. Later, to give the driver better visibility, it was moved to the left, and driving on the right became standard in most countries.

dismay and anger on the board of the Ford Motor Company. Yet another split was inevitable. By quick and ruthless wheeling and dealing, Ford bought out the directors who were opposed to his plan, including Malcolmson, and by November he owned 58% of the company's shares, giving him control of its activities. James Couzens, however, stayed.

Now, at last, Ford had achieved an ambition that he had nurtured since his departure from the Detroit Automobile Company. Then, as he wrote in his autobiography, "I resigned, determined never again to put myself under orders." He had had to break that pledge in order to survive in business – but now, finally, he was in a situation where he could call all the shots.

"All Ford"

Ford lost no time in expanding on his plans to the press. He wanted to gain the interest not only of the public who were his intended customers, but also of

businessmen in small towns across the United States who might be interested in becoming local Ford dealers. His new car would, he said, be "all Ford," meaning that every component would be supplied from within the Ford factory. This would not be the existing factory in Detroit where the company had started out, but a new one to be built on a sixty-acre (twenty-five-hectare) site on the old Highland Park racetrack just outside the city.

Then Henry gave his promise: "I will build a motor car for the great multitude. It will be large enough for the family but small enough for the individual to run and care for. It will be constructed of the best materials, by the best men to be hired, after the simplest designs that modern engineering can devise. But it will be so low in price that no man making a good salary will be unable to own one – and enjoy with his family the blessings of hours of pleasure in God's great open spaces."

The most surprising thing about Henry's announcement was that he planned to make only one model. Later, he was to announce an even more restrictive decision, his famous saying that "People can have any color they like, as long as it is black." This was against all the business opinion of the time, which argued that people wanted choice and would dig their heels in if they did not get it.

Developing a network

Between 1905 and 1907, with the help of a small team of engineers, Ford, now in his forties, worked away single-mindedly at the design of the new car and supervised the making of a half-scale model. This was tested, taken apart, put together again, and tested once more. A full-scale prototype, or trial model, followed. Ford tried it out on a hunting trip to Wisconsin with two of his engineer colleagues. They covered 1,357 miles (2183km) on sixty-eight gallons of fuel, driving about twenty miles to the gallon, which in those days was thought very economical. The Model T behaved well in this trial, and Henry ordered that his new factory should prepare for full-

Top: After many experiments, in 1908 Ford's workers built the first production Model T Ford, which Henry tried out on a hunting trip with friends. It took them successfully over 1,300 miles (2100km) through the forests of Wisconsin.

Above: Today's testing is more scientific. With monitors and sensors attached to the prototype car, it is given tests on technical performance, roadholding ability, comfort, and safety.

STRASBOURG
FORGE POUR LA FRANCE
LES MEILLEURES VOITURES DU MONDE
Ford MATHIS

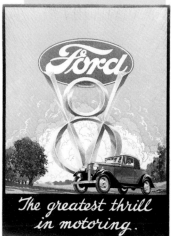

The greatest thrill in motoring.

Top: Henry Ford identified Europe, after North America, as the largest market for cars. Above: Models like the V8 were developed in response to the competition from other manufacturers whose cars may have seemed more exciting and innovative than Ford's.

scale production as soon as it was ready. At the same time, through advertisements and press interviews, he began his assault on the American public.

The Ford logo

The 1908 advertisement listed ten branches in the United States and one each in London, Paris (where a sales branch was established that year), and Toronto, where the Model T could be inspected and ordered. But this was only the beginning. Henry Ford wanted to make it as easy for rural Americans to buy a Model T as, say, a new pair of boots. The heart of his marketing plan was to set up a network of dealers, local businessmen with premises that would serve as a showroom, who would tie themselves exclusively to the Ford name, selling only Ford cars. The plan was that within the next five years there was to be a Ford dealer in every American town with a population of more than two thousand. Visibility was vital to sales. As soon as the Ford Motor Company had been established the distinctive Ford logo, which has altered very little since then, had been devised. Simple and unmistakable, short and memorable, it was another valuable marketing tool that gave Ford cars and the showrooms of Ford dealers a special character.

"The world on wheels"

Henry Ford did not confine his ambitions to the North American continent, but continued to build on the international links that had already been made. By 1910, when dealer networks were being set in place within the United States, Ford cars had reached Japan, Spain, and the Austro-Hungarian empire.

The first Ford factory outside the United States was set up in Manchester, England, in 1911 as a result of a growing demand for Ford's Model T. In the first year over three thousand were built. A French Ford assembly plant opened in Bordeaux in 1913. It began to look as if one of the early Model T advertising slogans – "the car that put the world on wheels" – was no idle boast.

"Tin Lizzie"

It was not long before the Model T acquired affectionate nicknames – among the most memorable the "Tin Lizzie" and "The Flivver." These were the first of many jokes that were to be made about the Model T – but Henry Ford didn't mind. Indeed, he quickly realized that jokes were free advertising. And although Americans might joke about Tin Lizzie, they still bought it. Henry's master-stroke had been to design a car that was suitable for the rough and rocky conditions of rural America. At that time, the best roads outside towns and cities were "dirt roads" with a two-inch layer of gravel on top of the bare earth. Away from these, the roads were mere farm tracks. With its high clearance and rugged construction, the Model T was unsurpassed at coping with these conditions. What was more, the design of its engine was so simple that a farmer or a farmhand with basic mechanical knowledge could cope with breakdowns.

Sales of the Model T during its first year were 10,607 at $850 each. Each year until 1913 production in the United States almost doubled the previous year's. The rest of America's car makers could only look on with a mixture of astonishment and envy.

The problems of success

This phenomenal success had, however, brought problems. It was good to have a runaway success – but Henry Ford worried about those customers who could not be supplied. Many of them, he knew, would go to another make of car, and possibly stay with it forever – or, in the case of farmers, buy another horse instead.

There were basically two difficulties. One was that the Ford company had become the victim of the success of its own promotion. The second was that the first Model Ts were still practically hand-built, a painfully slow method for a product in volume demand.

The Model T of 1925 was still recognizably the same car as the 1908 version and had another three years to go before production was stopped. Compared with other makes of car it was now dowdy and old-fashioned. People wanted the car they chose to say something about themselves as well as to get them from one place to another. Increasingly, it seemed as if Model T owners were admitting to being out of date or too poor to move upmarket.

Mass production

The breakthrough in solving this problem was the assembly of cars by mass production methods. Henry Ford is often thought of, wrongly, as the "father" of mass production. In fact, he was the first manufacturer to apply it to car assembly, but mass production itself was an industrial method whose use had been growing in the United States for well over one hundred years.

It began in 1798 with a firearms manufacturer, Eli Whitney, in New Haven, Connecticut. He was given an urgent United States government order for ten thousand muskets. In those days it was usual to make each gun by hand as a piece of craftsmanship, but the order was too large and too urgent to be handled in that way. Whitney built machine tools so accurate that they could duplicate the separate parts of the muskets identically. Instead of painstakingly fitting the parts of each individual gun together and making tiny adjustments with files and grindstones until they worked smoothly, muskets could be assembled quickly from interchangeable parts. There was an added bonus in this. If, in use, one part broke or was damaged, it could easily be replaced by an identical part from stock.

The United States Army was wary of Whitney's ideas, but the story is told of how he proved his point

Above and right: One of the key features of Ford's mass production system was to have supplies of parts for assembly delivered to the appropriate section of the production line. In today's heavily organized and computerized factories (opposite) the early principles of mass production still apply.

by assembling a musket at high speed from piles of assorted parts in front of the generals' eyes. Other gun manufacturers were quick to adopt Whitney's idea of interchangeable parts, and during the nineteenth century it spread to such industries as clock and watch making and the manufacture of sewing machines, typewriters, and bicycles. Compared with the assembly of a car, however, these were relatively simple devices, and all were easily portable from one workbench to the next. Mass production in the motor industry was a far greater challenge.

Taking work to the worker

The first principle of mass production, Ford wrote, is that "the work must be brought to the man, not the man to the work."

The moving assembly line was Ford's means of achieving this, but the idea was established long before Henry Ford was born. As early as 1738 an American miller, Oliver Evans, had devised an early form of assembly line – a chain of buckets that carried grain through his mill from its raw state to its emergence as sealed sacks of flour at the other end of the chain.

The importance of timing

The idea of accurately timing manufacturing operations – another essential feature of mass production – came from yet another American engineer, Frederick Winslow Taylor. He was a pioneer of what he called "scientific management." Taylor's theory was that productivity could be dramatically increased by studying, in minute detail, each operation carried out by a worker, noting every movement made. This could lead to simplifying operations by, for example, placing materials and parts in the most convenient position and so eliminating wasted effort and time. A development of Taylor's ideas was that, as the average time taken to carry out a particular task could be observed, the cost of the time spent on each task could be built into

an accurate estimate of the total cost of the work. The time could also be used to fix rates of pay for different tasks.

Taylor's ideas were hugely attractive to Ford. He incorporated many of them as he planned the mass production of cars at the new Highland Park plant.

Work on the assembly line was very monotonous, with the workers having to perform the same task hundreds of times a day. In this sub-assembly line at Highland Park, pictured here in 1914, flywheels were produced for the Model T.

Getting it together

The separate techniques of manufacturing that make up mass production came together gradually after Highland Park had gone into production. It took about seven years to reach the point where each operation was brought into the mass production process.

Ford hired an efficiency expert, Walter Flanders, who arranged for the work to be subdivided into twenty-nine separate small operations. Flanders stationed a group of unskilled workers, who had been trained only to perform their particular tasks, at points along a conveyor. This way, the time was cut down. From then on, Flanders moved from department to department, assessing the tasks, dividing them up, and setting up sub-assembly lines for each component.

Meanwhile, experiments were carried out on a main assembly line. In the first one, the chassis of a Model T was dragged through the factory by two men with a rope, parts being added as it moved along. The next experiment replaced the men with a horse and windlass. The results were impressive. The time taken to assemble a complete car fell from about twelve and a half hours to just under six.

Ford described the three principles of mass production as the planned orderly movement of the product through the factory, the delivery of work to the worker, and the careful analysis of manufacturing operations into their constituent parts. It was important that the work should be delivered to the worker at waist height to eliminate bending and stretching that were so wasteful of time and energy.

Value for money

The effect of the introduction of mass production at Highland Park was dramatic. In 1913, the number of Model Ts produced was 168,220, and in 1914 – the first year of full assembly line operation – it had increased to 248,307. The time required to assemble a Model T fell steadily until it reached an unheard-of ninety-three seconds. This was not good enough, Ford said. He wanted to produce a car every minute.

These production changes were accompanied by a steady fall in the price of the Model T. Each drop in the price, Ford knew well, brought more potential customers into the market. "Every time I reduce the charge for our car by one dollar," he claimed, "I get one thousand new buyers." He had beaten his own promise, back in 1908, to offer Americans a car for only $400 as they reached their lowest price of $260.

Supply and demand

The scale and speed of the Ford operation soon revealed flaws in the assembly system. Some suppliers could not keep up with the pace of Ford's

"The car of the future must be a car for people, a car that any man can own who can afford a horse and carriage; and mark my words, the car is coming sooner than most people think."

Henry Ford, 1910.

demand for parts. As a result, deliveries became erratic and there were hold-ups on the production line because parts had not arrived. Secondly, in their haste to keep up, some suppliers neglected their inspection procedures. Ford found that it was impossible to impose quality control standards on suppliers in their own factories, so Ford inspectors had to waste time re-inspecting deliveries and rejecting defective parts. The delays resulting from all this were resented by the time-conscious, value-for-money-conscious Henry Ford, and he began setting up subsidiary plants to make Ford's own parts.

Over the first few years of the Model T's production life, an increasing proportion of parts was made in Ford factories, leaving only special items to be bought in from outside the company. The Ford company became what is known in today's management language as a vertically integrated

The logical layout of a factory demanded by mass production methods calls for large sites. For this reason, car plants tend to be built on "greenfield" sites on the outskirts of cities, where land is plentiful and relatively cheap. Seen here are Ford's Flat Rock factory in Michigan, U.S.A. (left), and the Hermosillo factory in Mexico.

business, in which as many manufacturing processes as possible were carried out under direct company control. Ford's goal to produce parts "in house" was finally within his grasp.

The loss of a business partner

Henry Ford's business manager and colleague since 1903, James Couzens, was closely involved with any problems within the work force while the new assembly lines were being installed. Couzens and Ford, who almost came to blows over Ford's earlier wish to produce "all Ford" parts "in house," were both highly ambitious men, and both were jointly responsible for the success of the company. However, both men disagreed over crucial business decisions and plans.

The final break came over the two men's different ideas as to the role that Ford plants should play in the war efforts of World War I. In 1915, James Couzens left the Ford Motor Company, declaring that he could no longer work alongside Ford. He was later bought out of the company by the Ford family – his $900 investment made in 1903 had grown to a value of over $29 million.

A new president

Couzens' departure must have been unfortunate for the Ford Motor Company. But 1919 brought a newcomer to the head of the business from inside the family – Henry Ford's son, Edsel. Now twenty-six, Edsel became the company president. He had been brought up to expect that he would take his father's place as president of the Ford Motor Company. Edsel Ford and his wife, Eleanor Clay, already had a first son, Henry II, to continue the Ford line in the Ford Motor Company.

Edsel's appointment did not mean that his father was to lessen his involvement in the company, however. Henry Ford himself had already become something of a folk-hero to the American public – the story of a poor farmer's son who had brought everyday motoring to the "great multitude."

A generation gap

Ford continued to govern his company closely. His concern for his workers extended to their lifestyles. He used the internal publication channels to impress upon them how they should live their lives.

This paternalistic style of management had been fairly common in the nineteenth century. Employers often provided libraries, entertainments, reading rooms, and education and sports facilities for their workers. While Henry Ford did not go that far, he did set up good training facilities (a tradition that the Ford company has maintained), he established a hospital for Ford workers, and he went to some lengths to encourage outstanding young employees who had caught his eye. But such paternalism was out of date in the twentieth century, especially after the social upheavals of World War I which had made so many people – young people in particular – question the values of the previous generation.

The River Rouge plant, opened in 1919, fulfilled Henry Ford's dream of a fully integrated production site. Beside the Rouge river, it had docks for ships bringing raw materials and fuel, and was also alongside two major railway lines. It was a perfect example, on a huge scale, of Henry Ford's belief in "bringing the work to the worker."

"Our purpose is to construct and market an automobile for everyday wear and tear – business, professional, and family use ... a machine which will be admired by man, woman, and child alike for its compactness, its simplicity, its safety, its all-round convenience, and ... its exceedingly reasonable price."

Henry Ford, in his first advertisement for the Ford car.

River Rouge

Despite the changes brought about by the war, the popularity of the Model T grew. Demand had outstripped the resources of the Highland Park factory, and a completely new plant was opened in 1919 at River Rouge, six miles (10km) south west of Detroit. This had large docks, railway yards, storage for coke and ore, blast furnaces, coke ovens, and a foundry covering thirty acres (twelve hectares), which was at that time the largest in the world. Coke and ore arrived at River Rouge by ship and train. Steel was made and cylinder blocks, crankshafts, and other Ford parts were cast on the same site.

The site where Ford wanted to build the River Rouge plant was chosen carefully because of its potential to be self-sufficient and self-serving. However, the Detroit, Toledo and Ironton Railway ran straight through the proposed site. Henry Ford bought the railway because its right of way interfered with his plans. He was a man who would not be thwarted once he had made up his mind.

Economy of scale

With the Model T's popularity ever increasing, it was no wonder that it was so hugely profitable. It was a perfect example of what is known in business as economy of scale. Any new product that hits the market – the video, the compact disc player, even a new medicine – is expensive at first because all the costs of research, design, testing, and tooling up for production have to be paid for. If the product flops – as many do – those costs still have to be paid. But if the product succeeds like the Model T, the manufacturer can begin to reduce the selling price as sales rise and the "up front" costs are absorbed. With only minor changes, the Model T was in production from 1908 to 1927. The vast American market had enabled Ford to expand into Europe – still with the same car – and undercut any price that European manufacturers could offer. There was even, in the 1920s, a drive to sell Model Ts into the post-revolutionary U.S.S.R., despite the United States goverment's opposition to the U.S.S.R.'s Communist regime.

Above: Henry Ford was always single-minded in his actions and seldom allowed anyone or anything to get in the way. Despite its unpopularity with many Western countries, the Communist state of the Soviet Union became a new area for the export of Ford cars.

Zapping the dealers

To reach these expanding markets, Ford had built up an extensive Ford dealer network. The relationship between manufacturers and their distributors is a complex one of mutual dependence, relying on one another. The dealer has to face the customer, and so is in the first line of fire if there is anything wrong with the product. He has to rely on the manufacturer to deliver his promises. In turn, the manufacturer has to rely on the dealer to push his products and explore all the possibilities of making sales within his area. The success of the Model T had made very good

Left: When producing a new product, whether it is a Model T or a compact disc player, making a prototype, or test model, is an essential step. Once all the teething problems of the product have been dealt with, full-scale production can go ahead. If the product is a success, the business principle of economy of scale comes into action.

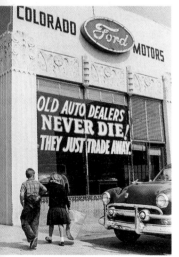

profits for the small-town businessmen who obtained Ford dealerships, and it was in the small towns of the midwestern and western United States that the Model T had its greatest triumphs.

But the dealers were vulnerable. A team of Ford company inspectors toured the territories, checking that dealers' premises were clean and tidy, that Ford promotion material was properly displayed, and sometimes even dropping in on Model T owners to ask their opinion of the local Ford outlet. At the same time, dealers' discounts, the allowances they got when buying the cars from Ford to sell on to the public, were trimmed. This forced them to sell more cars to make enough money to stay in business.

In 1920, following the end of the World War I boom in industry, an economic depression hit the United States, threatening the future of Ford as it threatened other prominent American companies. Borrowing heavily from the banks to stay in business, Ford needed cash quickly. Of all the factors in business, cash flow is one of the most vital. A company can be doing very well in theory, but unless there is a steady stream of money from sales, the company's debts to suppliers of parts and materials, and interest payments to the banks, cannot be paid. This was the situation Ford faced. Under the weight of the depression, sales figures plummeted. The flow of orders from customers to dealers, and from dealers to the Ford company, began to dry up.

A business decision

Ford's response was an astonishing piece of business gamesmanship. The Ford factories continued to turn out Model Ts at their usual pace, and these were sent out to dealers whether they had been ordered or not. When the dealers protested, they were told that unless they paid cash on delivery for the cars they had not wanted, plus the delivery charge, they would be struck off the Ford dealer network. This would, of course, have meant ruin, so they were forced to take out bank loans to pay the Ford bill. In this ingenious but ruthless way, Ford transferred his own bank debts to the dealers.

A change in fashion

In 1923, Model T production hit a peak of 2,011,125 – with one car being built every ten seconds – four and a half times the sales of the United States' second best-selling car, General Motors' Chevrolet. Because Ford had concentrated for fifteen years on one model, with only trivial changes from year to year, the company had been saved the expensive design and retooling costs that some rival car manufacturers, who believed in the need for a new model or at least a new look each year, had suffered.

But, as almost everyone in the Ford company recognized, except for Ford himself, times were changing. The Model T's time was up. Sales figures in 1925 told the story. Other manufacturers reported increased sales, but sales of the Model T fell by sixty thousand. Henry Ford, now aged sixty, still refused to accept the inevitable. But no matter how much pressure was put on the dealers, the writing was on the wall. In 1926, Model T production slumped by half a million. The United States now had its second generation of motorists, young people who wanted

Ford's main competitor in the American car market in the 1920s was General Motors, who produced a huge range of models. But it was the Chevrolet that Ford most feared. Below is a modern Chevrolet whose sporty image first began to threaten the Model T's supremacy in 1925.

something more exciting than the workhorse their parents drove. That something was the Chevrolet – the "Chevy" – whose sales figures, though still a long way behind, were remorselessly creeping up on the Model T's.

Refinements and accessories

The Chevy's appeal was not only that it had a younger image. It was also better equipped. If you bought a Model T, you got a very basic car to which you then had to add accessories, such as an electric self-starter and wheel trims. The Chevy came complete with these and other refinements. What was more, if you bought a Chevy you bought a car that had been designed in the past year or two. The Model T design had hardly been changed since 1908 – and looked it.

Ford dealers came to Detroit in great numbers to plead with Ford to replace the outdated model. A last-minute attempt was made in 1926 to breathe new life into "Tin Lizzie" by reducing its ground clearance and making it available in "fawn grey, gunmetal blue, phoenix brown and highland green." But Henry Ford finally accepted the truth that the Model T had come to the end of its useful life. On May 31, 1927, the 15,007,033rd and last Detroit-built Model T came off the assembly line at River Rouge. Production continued for a few more months at Ford's European assembly plants in England, Belgium, and Italy, but the company had finally said goodbye to the car that had made its name. The big problem was, of course, how to follow the Model T?

Never the same again

Tin Lizzie's successor was the Model A. Different from the Model A first introduced in 1903, its completely new design incorporated many of the features that rival manufacturers, taking advantage of Henry Ford's resistance to change, had already built into their cars. These included four-wheel brakes (the Model T had brakes on only two wheels); hydraulic shock absorbers, which made use of a piston inside a

In the 1930s, when competition and a fall in sales caused Ford to recognize a growing market for cars among young people, the Ford car started to reflect a need to become more fashionable, rather than just practical, in order to attract sales.

"We do not make changes for the sake of making them, but we never fail to make a change once it is demonstrated that the new way is better than the old way."

Henry Ford, from Ford in Europe.

cylinder of oil to smooth out the ride over bumpy road surfaces, and the use of a safety-glass for the windows and wipers.

The Model A sold well – production began with an order book of 727,000 – but it had nothing like the success of Tin Lizzie. The Chevrolet and a newcomer, Chrysler's Plymouth saloon, were challenging Ford in the North American market. In Europe, competition was even fiercer, with the French companies Peugeot, Citroen, and Renault, the

Renault was founded in France by the three Renault brothers, and soon became one of the country's leading car makers. Originally, Renault followed Ford's ideas and aimed to produce a small, cheap, reliable car. Their advertising, as this example from the 1930s shows, was less descriptive but more elaborate than Ford's.

Italian Fiat, and the British Austin and Morris companies all fighting for a significant place in a growing market. Ford would remain a leading player in the motor industry but it would never again be able to claim undisputed leadership in the popular car sector. The industry of the 1920s was very different from that of the early years of the century.

A union ban

Ford had proved that he was a determined businessman. He was going to achieve his vision of the car industry and nothing was going to stand in his way. Where unions threatened to disrupt his work force, he banned them from his factories.

Unions are organizations of workers who join together to protect workers' rights. Ford did not want this sort of organization working within his business. He argued that, coming from humble origins himself, he knew what was best for his employees. Despite United States laws authorizing unions in industrial plants, Henry Ford held out against them. The Ford work force was denied the protection from exploitation that it badly needed. There was instant dismissal for any worker who could not keep up with the pace of the assembly line. Talking, unless it was essential to the work, was forbidden.

Mass production and stress

The dramatic changes in the way the company was set up in terms of the day-to-day work on the assembly line caused inevitable problems. Changes in the way people are expected to work produce tensions among a company's work force. This was seen in the 1970s and 1980s with the introduction of computers into almost every aspect of working life, resulting in the loss of many jobs and the retraining of millions of other workers. The same had been true a century before Henry Ford's time when steam-operated spinning and weaving machines replaced hand-powered processes and thousands of workers in the textile industry had to adapt to learning new skills or face unemployment. The switch from hand assembly to mass production in the car industry brought similar stresses.

Craftsmen who built cars from start to finish, in small groups, could take pride in their work, and had the "job satisfaction" of seeing the car they had assembled as a team roll out of the workshop. They could also relate to each other as individuals, valuing their own and their teammates' skills. The assembly

Over the past two hundred years, many old skills, like this use of hand-looms, have been replaced by automation and, more recently, computerization.

As job satisfaction was threatened by the advancement of production line work, it became increasingly important to attract new workers. In 1914, Henry Ford announced the doubling of the minimum daily wage for his workers to five dollars (£1.25). It was an unprecedented amount for a company to pay unskilled employees who had been trained only for a repetitive task.

line robbed workers of these compensations. It was hard for a worker to take any pride in what he did, or obtain any satisfaction from it, if his only function was to fit a nut to a bolt that would be tightened by the next worker down the line.

The meaning of work

Such changes caused great concern in the industrial world of the 1920s and 1930s about the increased "meaninglessness" of people's working lives, as so many old craft skills were replaced by unskilled machine-minding. This ran alongside concern about the changes occurring as large numbers of people left the countryside to find better-paid factory work in the cities. Ford could be classed as a hard and sometimes insensitive employer, but he could hardly be blamed for the tide of social change that was sweeping across the industrial world. The decline of traditional crafts and the rush of people to the cities had been going on for well over a century, and the car industry was only reflecting trends that were already established in other industries. He was not slow to point out that when farm workers gave up their jobs and came to Detroit to find work in his factory, they showed no sign of wishing they were back on the farm.

There were other disturbing aspects of work on the assembly line, however. In a small engineering workshop, employees were able to work, within reason, at the pace they chose. It was true that a foreman might come and tell them to work a bit faster, but at least he was a human being who could be reasoned with. On an assembly line, the speed of the main assembly track dictates the pace of work. The individual worker has no control. If production needs to be increased, the assembly line can be set to travel faster, this can be a source of stress and discontent. When Ford workers saw Henry Ford announcing yet another cut in the price of the Model T, they knew perfectly well that it had been at least partly achieved by their having to do more work for the same money.

The inevitable explosion came in 1937, when members of the union, called the United Automobile Workers of America, planned to hand out membership leaflets one May afternoon as Ford workers came off their shift. It was to prove one of the blackest days in the history of American workers and one that was not easily forgotten.

The battle of River Rouge

The union men took up their position on a footbridge linking the River Rouge factory with a bus stop. They were met by members of a Detroit street gang, hired, it was said, by the company, who warned them off. Protesting, the union members left, to run straight into another gang of hired heavies who began to beat them up.

Press photographers at the scene had their cameras snatched and their film destroyed, but enough escaped to expose the scenes of violence in the following day's papers.

Over the next few weeks, there were similar scenes at other Ford plants. The company's treatment of the unions and its workers became a national scandal, and the government's National Labor Relations Board issued a stern warning to Ford. Eventually, Henry Ford gave way and allowed unions into Ford factories.

Following page: In developing the Fordson tractor, Henry Ford applied the same principles to farming equipment as he had to the development of the small family car. The Fordson made tractor ownership possible for millions of small farmers worldwide. Since it first came onto the market in 1907, the Fordson has undergone many changes and made a lasting contribution to agriculture.

A dispute erupts as Ford workers demonstrate against their working conditions at the River Rouge factory.

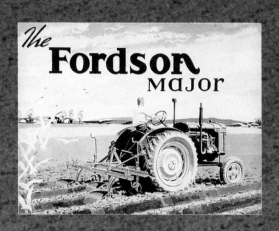

The Fordson Major

Broader horizons

Perhaps Henry Ford, now in his seventies, recognized that the motor industry was no longer the same industry that he had helped to shape at the beginning of the twentieth century.

He began to spread his interests in other directions. He tried, unsuccessfully, to take a controlling interest in a hydroelectric power project. He set up an aircraft production company. He built a model village and museum to celebrate his own background, and even took up an interest in traditional square dancing, with a full-time dance instructor and a band on the payroll.

Independently of the Ford Motor Company, he set up a company to make tractors specifically for the small farmer. The Fordson, as it was called, became an instant success, repeating on a smaller scale the triumphs of the Model T.

Father and son

Edsel's presidency had continued to be very much overshadowed by his father. However, Edsel remained loyal to both Henry Ford and the business, visiting European plants and enforcing business plans. By 1934, Ford had assembly plants in France, Belgium, Italy, Britain, Germany, and Spain. However, in 1943, the Ford Company suffered a blow – at the age of forty-nine, Edsel died from stomach cancer.

The United States was then two years into World War II and relied heavily on Ford plants for the production of military vehicles and aircraft. Edsel's son Henry Ford II, Edsel's natural successor, was serving in the United States Navy. In Henry Ford senior's view, there was only one man who could step into the presidency – himself.

By this time, the Ford Motor Company was at the lowest point in its history. The eighty year old Henry, despite his continuing enthusiasm, no longer had the strength to manage the company. There were real fears that it might collapse.

In resuming the presidency of Ford, Henry was reckoning without the power of two strong women, his wife, Clara, and Edsel's widow, Eleanor. Eleanor, who had inherited Edsel's shares, now had voting rights in the company. Between them, the two women arranged for Henry Ford II to be released from the Navy and then began to campaign for Henry to hand over the presidency to him. It took two years. Finally, in 1945, Henry Ford II became president and his grandfather stepped down for the last time.

Father of the motor industry

On April 7, 1947, Henry Ford died at his home in Dearborn. At the time of his death there is said to have been a power cut so that his house was lit by kerosene lamps and candles, creating a scene similar to that of his birth eighty-three years earlier.

It is no exaggeration to say that few men can have
had such an influence on the way people's lives had
changed within his own lifetime. He was born into a
world where most travel was still dominated by
the horse and where steam-powered travel was
still a wondrous new invention. His technical
understanding, which was phenomenal considering
that he was entirely self-educated as an engineer,
enabled him to grasp the new technology of the
internal combustion engine and move it forward in
terms of performance.

A vision that was completely his own inspired him
to apply the new technology to the needs of the
people he knew best and from whence he came – the
"great multitude" of ordinary folk with whom he
grew up and whose lives, he perceived, could be made
easier and more satisfying by mechanization. The

One of Henry Ford's main aims was to make the car available to the multitude. Partly as a direct consequence, motoring has changed people's way of life and their environment. The development of fast roads – beautiful to some, but an eyesore to others – punctuates the countryside like this network of major roads at "Spaghetti Junction" near Birmingham, England (below left). New businesses, such as drive-in fast food outlets, reflect the changing needs of a motoring society (below right).

often-quoted claim that Henry Ford "put the world on wheels" is absolutely justified. His contribution to the industrial and social life of the twentieth century was unique.

Bringing Ford back to life

The company that Henry Ford II had inherited in 1945 was in bad shape. In the United States, it had concentrated mainly on war production for four years, to the neglect of its commercial markets. In continental Europe, many of its factories had been shattered by air raids or battle, and those that stayed in production were again geared to war work. In countries like Britain, there was a desperate post-war shortage of all kinds of raw materials, and the supply of new cars lagged well behind demand.

In 1946, Ford advertising invited readers to look into the company's crystal ball for a vision of the future. The "super de luxe" dream car was a long way from Henry Ford's original concept, but the world of motoring had changed, and the Ford Motor Company had to change with it.

Throughout the Ford factories in the United States and Europe, research and development had been interrupted by the war, and when car production resumed it was of models that had been introduced in 1939 or even before.

Added to this, in Europe, a problem was posed by the way Ford's European operations had developed piecemeal, or bit by bit, country by country. The result was that some European companies even competed against each other in the same markets with rival dealer networks. This was a waste of corporate, or company, energy and robbed Ford in Europe of the chance of making economies of scale by producing large numbers of cars suitable for all continental markets.

The Model T's legacy

But the years of prosperity with the Model T had given the Ford company the power and confidence to fight for its place in the market. It had a huge customer base, dating back nearly twenty years, of people who had never owned any car but a Ford. The loyalty of Ford owners was carefully nourished by national and local publicity. And there was still room for expansion, for Ford and its rivals, in the United States and overseas.

Henry Ford II was only twenty-eight when he became president. He was well aware of his inexperience. Some of the years he would normally have spent learning the business had been taken up with war service.

His solution was to bring in an experienced team to support him. The newcomers were from outside the car industry. They were "new brooms," university-trained professional managers, who questioned every one of the Ford company's long-standing business methods.

A climate of change

By the mid-1970s it was becoming clear that the entire motor industry was changing. Competition had opened up – there were too many manufacturers, including relative newcomers from Japan, chasing too few customers. This led to cooperation in joint product development between rival companies. For example, Ford of Europe developed production links for certain models with Volkswagen of Germany, and with the Japanese car maker Nissan, while in America Ford built up an association with the Japanese Mazda company.

Japanese car manufacturers have become a growing threat to Ford and other American companies since the 1960s, capturing a large slice of the family car market. In the 1990s, Ford began to work with, rather than compete against, the Japanese car industry, sharing deals with the Mazda company. In 1994, Ford launched a financial support package for Japanese Ford dealers and customers.

*Over ninety years of Fords
– the 1908 Model T, the
1934 Model Y and the
1992 Escort – show the
extensive changes in motor
car design that have kept
Ford one step ahead of its
competitors.*

These links produced cars that were identical in engineering terms but were given distinctive names, badges, trim, and accessories by the partner companies which marketed them individually. It is now possible to think in terms of a "world car," as Ford did with its Mondeo, launched in 1993.

The modern motor trade

The structure of the motor industry was not the only way in which the motor trade changed. Every step in the production of a new car, from the earliest design stages to final assembly and testing, was revolutionized by the computer. Drawing boards, on which teams of designers produced drawings of thousands of individual car parts, were replaced by VDU screens on which designs can be made and modified at the touch of a light pen.

**"The competitive road
ahead will be challenging.
But I want to assure
everyone that whatever
comes our way, there will
continue to be a Ford in
your future."**

*Ian Trotman, chairman of Ford,
June 15, 1994.*

Ford engineers were able to exchange information with their colleagues around the world through a database system that the company developed independently. The "Worldwide Engineering Release System" was believed to be the world's largest privately-owned database network. It provided essential design information, enabling engineers to call up working drawings to their computer terminals.

On the production line, computer-controlled robots perform many of the operations that were formerly done by hand or by workers using hand-held machine tools. On the Ford Mondeo, for example, 95% of the 3,400 welds on the bodyshell were made using robot control.

Above: Today, cars are designed on screen, with aerodynamics and other vital aspects of performance being assessed by computer.

With safety in mind

The budget for expenditure in new projects in the British market in 1993 was more than £2 billion. Research and development was an area of great concern to the company both in terms of new products and the safety standards of the cars that made it to production. In the United States, Ford was one of the first car companies to start crash-testing vehicles. By 1994, technology had taken the place of some actual crash-testing, whereby crashes could be simulated on screen and the type of damage assessed.

Also by early 1994, airbags had become a standard safety feature on certain Ford models, including the popular "compact" car, the Fiesta.

Below: In the event of a severe collision, an airbag will automatically inflate and cushion the head and face of the driver from injury.

Caring for the environment

Passenger safety aside, care for the environment was one of the company's oldest concerns, stemming from Henry Ford's own dislike of unnecessary waste and his interest in the countryside. Ford promoted recycling within his plants from an early stage. By the 1990s, the Ford company was sponsoring the worldwide Conservation Awards, run by the Conservation Foundation, a scheme that invited organizations to enter conservation projects into a Europe-wide competition.

In terms of the motor car, a high polluter itself, Ford spent much time and research on new ways to cut fume emissions. European regulations called for the fitting of catalytic converters to the exhaust systems of all new cars made since the early 1990s. Ford also investigated further measures that could be taken to reduce the pollution created by cars, considering ventures such as electrically run cars. In addition, it has looked into producing cars that are over eighty per cent recyclable.

A world market

The Ford Motor Company has changed internally as well. To eliminate the danger of becoming too "piecemeal," or fragmented, as it had been in Europe between the wars, the Ford company decided to try to "globalize."

In 1993, plans were put into motion, under the Chairmanship of Alan Trotman, to unite the production of Ford Europe and Ford America, and ultimately to link production worldwide. This was a new step forward since it meant that certain plants

Above: Transportation by water saves fuel, reduces road and rail traffic, and cuts down pollution. Ford won the Austrian Environmental Protection Prize in 1994 for carrying new cars from Germany to Austria by this method, on the River Danube.

Opposite: Conservation and care for the environment has come to be of utmost importance since the 1980s. Ford has also supported conservation projects and awards in Europe.

would be responsible for producing particular models of cars for the worldwide market, not just for specific countries as before. Such a change would eliminate the duplication of designs, make better use of resources, and the company would be able to move toward a "single set of worldwide processes and systems in its product development, manufacturing, supply and sales activities."

Such goals were not too far away from Henry Ford's original dream. Ford had been an international company since soon after its formation in 1903, when Henry Ford sold his Model A to Canada. Within ten or so years his company was selling cars throughout Europe, the United States, and Asia. In 1994, Ford had plants or other facilities in thirty countries, selling into more than two hundred markets, with a work force of nearly 340,000 people worldwide.

The changing faces of Ford. By adapting to change, Ford was as successful in the 1990s (top) as it was in the heady days of Model T production (above).

Important dates

1863   July 30: Henry Ford is born to William and Mary Ford, at Greenfield, Michigan, in the United States.

1876   Henry's mother, Mary Ford, dies in childbirth.

1879   Henry Ford leaves home and walks to Detroit to find work.

1882   Henry Ford completes his apprenticeship as a mechanic in Detroit.

1884   Henry Ford, aged twenty-one, returns to Greenfield to manage woodland given to him by his father.

1888   April 11: Henry Ford marries Clara Bryant.

1891   Henry and Clara Ford move to Detroit and Henry starts work with the Detroit Edison Electricity Company. In his spare time he begins to design his first car.

1893   Nov. 6: The Fords' first son, Edsel Bryant Ford, is born.

1896   June: Henry Ford's first car, the Quadricycle, makes its first run.

1899   Aug. 19: The Detroit Automobile Company is founded by William Murphy, with Henry Ford as its chief engineer.

1900   Nov. The Detroit Automobile Company closes.

1901   The Henry Ford Company is formed.
Oct. 10: Henry Ford becomes American motor-racing champion.

1902   The Henry Ford Company closes.

1903   June 16: The Ford Motor Company is formed, with Alexander Malcolmson as president and Henry Ford as vice-president.
The Model A Ford is launched in the U.S.A. and exported to Great Britain.

1904   The First Model A is sold in Canada and Australia.
The Ford Motor Company establishes a base in Canada.

1905   Ford announces the Model T to the American press.

1908   The Model T goes into production and sells in the United States, London, and Paris.

1911   The first overseas plant for producing Model Ts is established in Britain, at Trafford Park, Manchester.

1912   The first European Ford parts depot opens in Hamburg, Germany.

1913   The first Ford assembly plant is opened in Bordeaux, France.

1915   James Couzens leaves the Ford Motor Company.

1917   The first Ford truck, or Fordson, is produced.
Henry Ford II is born to Edsel and Eleanor Ford.

1919   A new Ford plant opens at River Rouge, near Detroit. Edsel Ford becomes nominal president of the Ford Motor Company.

1926   Sales of Model Ts slump by half a million dollars.

1927   May 31: Ford announces the end of Model T production.
Oct.: The last Model T is produced at River Rouge.

1937   May: The "Battle of River Rouge" – union protests – take place at many Ford plants.

1941   The United States enters World War II, and Ford factories are converted to war production.

1943   Edsel Ford dies from stomach cancer. Henry Ford again becomes president of the Ford Motor Company.

1945 Henry Ford II becomes president of the Ford Motor Company, and Henry Ford Senior finally retires.

1947 April 7: Henry Ford dies, aged eighty-three.

1959 The fifty-millionth Ford vehicle is produced.

1976 Ford's new European small car, the Fiesta, is introduced.

1979 Ford establishes links with the Japanese motor company Mazda.

1987 Henry Ford II dies.
Ford establishes links with the German motor company Volkswagen.

1993 Ford's "world car," the Mondeo, is launched.

1994 The safety feature of airbags becomes standard in many Ford models, including the Fiesta.
Nissan dealers agree to sell Ford cars in Japan.

Glossary

Assembly line: An arrangement, in mass production factories, whereby machines and workers put together the parts of a *product* step by step as it travels through the factory.

Autocrat: Someone in authority who insists on ruling in his own way.

Boycott: To refuse to have any dealings with a *company,* for example by not buying their *product,* and therefore excluding them from the *market.*

Capital: The amount of surplus money that a *company* or an individual has.

Consumer: A person who buys services or *products;* the customer.

Commercial: Concerned with commerce, or the exchange of goods through buying and selling.

Company: A group of two or more people that is registered to carry out a trade or business. A company is obliged to conform to certain regulations, which may vary from country to country or in the U.S.A. from state to state.

Dividend: In business, the sum of money paid out of the *company profits* to company *shareholders.* It is usually paid out once or twice a year.

Enterprise: An innovative idea in business.

General Manager: A person who is elected to organize and lead a *company.* He or she is responsible for making critical decisions that will help the company achieve its business goals.

Hydroelectric: The production of electricity by water power.

Innovative: Having new and creative ideas.

Investors: People who make a financial *investment* in a *company.*

Investment: When money, time or effort is put into something, for example setting up a business or buying a house, in the hope that it will result in a profit in the long term.

Manufacturer: A business or *company* responsible for the production of goods on a large scale, usually using machinery.

Market: In terms of a *company's* sales plan, the number of people who might want to buy a particular *product;* it also means to sell the product in an organized and preplanned way.

Mass market: Describing a *product* that appeals to a large number of people.

Overheads: In business, general expenses, or costs that do not belong to a particular department, such as heating and rent.

Paternalistic: Behaving in a fatherly way to other people, in this case employees.

Pioneer: Someone who originates new ideas.

Product: An item that is either manufactured or naturally produced.

Profit: The amount of money a *company* or individual has left over in a business venture after costs and expenses have been paid.

Profit margin: The area of *profit,* in a *company.*

Prototype: A model product that is used for testing so that necessary changes can be made before it is manufactured *commercially.*

Recruitment: Seeking out new members to join a *company.*

Share: An equal part of a *company's capital,* that can be bought and owned by a member of the company or *shareholder,* who is then entitled to a percentage of the company's profits.

Shareholder: Someone who owns *shares* in a *company.*

Showroom: A room set aside to display the goods for sale.

Stock market: The place where *shares* in different *companies* are bought and sold.

Windlass: A machine used for raising weights.

Index